aragettes"

ternut
uash
o with
cream

blasted
broccoli
and grape
tomatoes

cand...
cane...
cream

tomato
bonbons

rib-eye
roast in the style
of gravlax

pistachio-
crusted chilean
sea bass

shell-roasted
oysters,
black caviar
pearls

olive
oil mashed
potatoes

me
f beef,
rnet-
"jus"

heavenly
chocolate
cake

angels and
archangels on
horseback

sage-roasted
capon with
wild
mushrooms

s"

wild rice
with five-hour
onions

sugar
snaps in
orange
butter

pineapple
"au caramel"

bracing
ginger
ice milk

Christmas 1-2-3

three-ingredient holiday recipes

ROZANNE GOLD

STEWART, TABORI & CHANG
NEW YORK

Published in 2002 by
Stewart, Tabori & Chang
A Company of La Martinière Groupe
115 West 18th Street
New York, NY 10011

Export Sales to all countries
except Canada, France,
and French-speaking Switzerland:
Thames and Hudson Ltd.
181A High Holborn
London WC1V 7QX
England

Canadian Distribution:
Canadian Manda Group
One Atlantic Avenue, Suite 105
Toronto, Ontario M6K 3E7
Canada

Library of Congress Cataloging-in-Publication Data

Gold, Rozanne, 1954
    Christmas 1-2-3 : three ingredient holiday recipes / Rozanne Gold.
        p. cm.
    ISBN 1-58479-242-6
Christmas cookery. 2. Quick and easy cookery. I. Title

TX739.2.C45 G64 2002
641.5'68—dc21

2002075997

The text of this book was composed in The Sans
Designed by Galen Smith and Nicole Salzano

Printed in China.

10 9 8 7 6 5 4 3 2 1
First Printing

This cookbook brings great holiday tidings: It proclaims that a time of joy and celebration should never be thwarted by attempts to perform unrealistic culinary feats. So rejoice. My gift to cooks everywhere is a repertoire of simple and sumptuous holiday dishes bursting with the flavors of the season. These eighty-six recipes—each made with only three ingredients—fulfill the promise of abundance without the burden. Concentrate on the simple techniques behind each recipe, and you will have splendid results. During Christmas, when homes across America come alive with the spirit of the season, no one escapes its magic—except, perhaps, the cook. For even the most surefooted cooks have to deal with the special circumstances of the holidays: too many meals to make, too many people to feed, and too many guests gridlocked in the kitchen.

I say, keep it simple.
My approach elegantly compresses the tasks of shopping, prepping, and cooking, thereby giving the cook the most valuable gift of all: more time to enjoy the warmth of family and friends.

contents

holiday style

Tucked away next to your Christmas ornaments are, no doubt, the good silverware and fine china, the oversized wine goblets and your best linens. Use them. For larger parties you may need to rent extra things, but part of the magic of the holidays is incorporating objects that have been part of your family for generations.

Color and sparkle are de rigueur at the holiday table. It doesn't require great exertion to create three-ingredient centerpieces: tangerines with strings of fresh cranberries and lemon leaves; a pyramid of seasonal lady apples and Seckel pears with evergreen sprigs tucked in-between; a bowl of gold-sprayed pine cones, tiny red roses, and boughs of holly; or a dozen flickering votive candles illuminating your table. But the easiest way to add vibrancy to your table is to choose recipes that sport the colors of the season: a wreath of cut radishes nesting in their leaves; sausages "al vino" with red and green grapes; slow-roasted crimson tomatoes in a bed of emerald-green watercress; and on Christmas morning, a cut-crystal bowl of brilliant red strawberries aglitter with mint sugar looking like freshly fallen snow.

Although each of the recipes is complete, you can add more color and drama by using one of nature's own holiday garnishes: branches of fresh rosemary, bunches of sage tied with raffia, garlands of kumquats with their leaves, fresh bay leaves, little green and red hot peppers strung like Christmas lights, tiny clusters of champagne grapes, unsprayed lemon or grape leaves, sections of pomegranates that reveal edible seeds sparkling like jewels, whole roasted chestnuts, or cherry tomatoes still on their vine.

make it merry

Organization is key to a successful holiday meal, so choose dishes like Christmas Gravlax, Butternut Squash Soup with Leek Cream, and Heavenly Chocolate Cake that can be prepared days ahead, or wonderful side dishes like Wild Rice with Five-Hour Onions, Red Cabbage with Honey and Vinegar, and Sweet Potato–Ginger Puree that can be prepped early in the day and gently reheated.

Since Christmas is all about honoring tradition, these recipes are by no means meant to replace those dishes you and your family hold dear. Use them instead to augment the bounty of your holiday offerings, or to create new traditions.

With the hassles of shopping and the manipulation of many ingredients gracefully streamlined, I guarantee this will be your merriest Christmas ever.

the magic of three

When cooking with only three ingredients, each must be strongly expressed and, like the primary colors in a painting, the harmony among them can result in a richly layered experience. As I have demonstrated in my previous cookbooks, less is often more.

This concept applies beautifully to the holiday table, where every dish is meant to be special. So there are show-stoppers like Salmon Baked in a Golden Balloon and Prime Ribs of Beef with Cabernet-Garlic "Jus." And easy-to-make but lavishly flavored dishes, including snowy sea bass swathed in pesto under a mantle of pistachios, a pomander-roasted turkey filled with those clove-studded oranges that some folks use as decorations, and bay-smoked Châteaubriand in an amber Marsala reduction.

And there are wonderful twists on old standards: a cinnamon-sugar crust for the holiday ham, a novel way to prepare a rib-eye roast, succulent pork loin stuffed with plump apricots, and a golden goose filled with seasonal chestnuts and dried plums. There is even a trendy wasabi-glazed salmon that can be prepped in three minutes. All with just three ingredients.

My philosophy is simple enough: Let the flavors of the best ingredients shine bright. Whether trendy or traditional, the magic of three applies not just to the recipes but to the spirit of the season—so I wish you peace on earth, good will toward men, and a joyful kitchen.

ingredients & equipment

When cooking "my way," every ingredient counts—except salt, pepper, and water—so buy the finest products and treat them with respect. That's the golden rule of simple cooking.

Simplicity also rules when it comes to equipment. My kitchen is airy and spacious but quite low-tech. I use a food processor and blender quite often, but I don't own a microwave oven. I have a variety of pots, pans, and casseroles, but nothing fancy. I do have a standing mixer, a sturdy roasting pan, and meat thermometer, which I use regularly. Read each recipe carefully before you start cooking to make sure you have what you need.

Of course you'll want special cookie cutters for making Snowy Shortbread and festive tins for storing all of your holiday treats.

christmas
hors d'oeuvres

Radish Wreath with Goat Cheese
and Toasted Cumin

Angels and Archangels on Horseback

Spiced Shrimp in Sweet Rice Wine

Brie Croustades with Red Caviar

"Asparagettes"

Red Pepper Frittata Bites

Smoked Salmon in Pillows

Cherry Tomato Bonbons

Hot and Crispy Cheese Truffles

a few quick and easy hors d'oeuvres

Golden Almonds with Dill

Stuffed Olives in Sweet Vermouth

Fried Chickpeas
with Walnut Oil and Sage

Peppery Pecans

Tomato-Anisette "Demitasse"

Tiny Oysters
with Champagne Mignonette

Quesadillas with
Fontina and Truffle Oil

Foie Gras "Kisses"

radish wreath with goat cheese and toasted cumin

These little radishes, adapted from my book Entertaining 1-2-3, *are as crisp as a winter's morning. With its intriguing flavors and stunning simplicity, it was chosen as one of the "Best Recipes of 2000" and included in a best-selling cookbook. The stark red-and-white radishes placed in a circular fashion atop dark green radish leaves look like an edible wreath.*

18 medium red radishes, round as possible, with stems and leaves

6 ounces fresh goat cheese

2 tablespoons cumin seeds

Wash radishes and leaves well. Dry thoroughly and cut leaves from radishes, leaving 1 inch of stem attached to each radish. Remove any spindly roots. Refrigerate leaves until ready to use. Cut radishes in half through the root end and cut a tiny slice from their rounded bottoms so they don't wobble.

Place cheese in a food processor with 1½ tablespoons water. Process until smooth, being careful not to overprocess. Mixture should be creamy and very thick. Using a small knife, spread cheese thickly on cut side of each radish. Or put cheese in a pastry bag with a large star tip, and pipe onto each radish. Refrigerate briefly until ready to serve.

Arrange radish leaves on a platter to make a wreath shape (a wide circle with a hole in the center). Place radishes on leaves.

In a small nonstick skillet, toast cumin and ½ teaspoon salt over medium heat until cumin darkens a bit and the aroma rises. Sprinkle each radish with toasted cumin.

MAKES 36 PIECES

angels and archangels on horseback

Once upon a time oysters were so plentiful that they had very little value and were considered "the food of the poor." Yet in traditional English homes, Angels on Horseback were served at the end of the meal, after desserts, as a "savory" to neutralize the sugar taste before port was served. When scallops are substituted, the dish is known as Archangels on Horseback. (Archangels are angels of particularly high rank.)

8 thin slices white bread

24 fresh large oysters or medium sea scallops

12 thin slices bacon

Preheat the oven to 450 degrees. Remove crusts from bread and save for another use. Cut 1½-inch circles from bread, using a cookie cutter. Toast lightly on both sides in the oven and set aside.

Pat the oysters or scallops dry and season with freshly ground black pepper. Cut the bacon strips in half and wrap each strip around an oyster or scallop. Secure tightly with toothpicks. Place on a baking sheet. Bake for 10 minutes. Remove the picks and serve on the toasts.

SERVES 6 TO 8

A FANCY TWIST

Instead of the bread, spread a little apple butter on each scallop, wrap in bacon, and secure with a small bamboo skewer. Bake for 10 minutes and serve hot.

spiced shrimp in sweet rice wine

This will no doubt become one of your "new culinary traditions" to serve with holiday cocktails. Large shrimp are gently cooked in a dulcet bath of sweet rice wine (known as mirin) and aromatics to create a lovely synergy of sweet, salty, and spice.

24 very large shrimp in shells, about 1¼ pounds

½ cup mirin (Japanese sweet rice wine)

2 heaping tablespoons pickling spice

Place the shrimp in a medium pot. Add mirin, pickling spice, and 1½ cups cold water or enough to barely cover shrimp. Add 2½ teaspoons salt and bring just to a boil.

Cover pot and cook over low heat only until shrimp turn pink and lose their translucence, about 2 minutes. Remove from heat and let shrimp cool in the liquid. Taste and adjust seasonings, adding more mirin or salt as needed. Refrigerate until very cold.

Drain shrimp with a slotted spoon and pile high in a bowl, leaving your guests to peel the shrimp themselves. Provide small bowls for shells. Or peel the shrimp, leaving the tails intact, and arrange them on a decorative plate.

SERVES 6

NICE TOUCH
Serve with tiny pumpernickel bread-and-butter sandwiches.

brie croustades with red caviar

Two simple ingredients are magically transformed into golden cups that welcome lustrous coral beads of slightly salty salmon eggs. Served barely warm, they make a compelling contrast with chilled caviar. For an optional garnish, you can hard-boil an additional egg, sieve the yolk and finely chop the white, and sprinkle either, or both, over the caviar.

½ pound double-cream Brie cheese, chilled

3 extra-large eggs

½ cup salmon caviar

Cut rind from cheese using a small sharp knife. Discard rind. Let cheese sit at room temperature for 30 minutes. Meanwhile, preheat the oven to 350 degrees.

Put eggs in bowl of a food processor. Cut cheese into 1-inch pieces and add to processor. Process until very smooth and thick, about 1 minute.

Coat two 12-hole 2-inch-diameter nonstick muffin pans with cooking spray. Spoon 1 tablespoon cheese mixture into each muffin cup. Bake for 9 to 10 minutes, until croustades are puffed and golden.

Let croustades sit for 1 minute, then remove from tins using a small flexible spatula. Top each slightly warm or room-temperature croustade with 1 teaspoon caviar. (Before topping with caviar, the croustades can be rewarmed: place in a pie pan, cover with foil, and heat for 3 minutes in a 325-degree oven. Serve within 20 minutes.)

MAKES 24

"asparagettes"

These look like cigarettes, hence the name. Slim asparagus spears are blanched, then rolled in tissue-paper-thin sheets of phyllo dough, doused with basil-scented oil, and baked until the pastry is crackly. Addictive!

36 medium-thin
asparagus spears

12 (12-by-17-inch)
sheets phyllo dough

½ cup basil oil *

Cut off the top 3 inches of each asparagus spear. (Reserve the rest for another use.) Bring a pot of salted water to a boil. Add asparagus tips and cook for 3 to 4 minutes, until bright green and just beginning to get tender. Drain immediately under cold water. Pat dry. You may prepare up to this point and refrigerate.

Preheat the oven to 375 degrees. Cut each sheet of phyllo into 6 rectangles. Using a pastry brush, moisten 36 rectangles with basil oil. Place an unoiled piece on top of each oiled rectangle.

Pat each asparagus tip dry and season with salt and pepper. Place each asparagus tip on the edge of each phyllo stack and roll up tightly, brushing with oil as you go. The result should look like a fat cigarette.

Brush with more oil and sprinkle lightly with salt. Place on a baking sheet and bake for 15 minutes, turning twice during baking. Remove from oven when pastry is crisp and golden. Serve immediately. If desired, serve with a little bowl of salted basil oil, for dipping.

MAKES 36

*Good-quality basil oils can be found in most supermarkets and specialty food stores.

red pepper frittata bites

Rarely do I use prepared products, but the sweet pepper slices you can buy in a jar (B&G is a good brand) are perfect for these eggy little squares. The vinegar from their marinade gives the egg mixture a firm yet custardy texture. Very sharp cheddar cheese, preferably a good farmhouse cheddar from England or an artisanal cheese from Vermont, will elevate your effort. Serve the bites warm or at room temperature and decorate with something green, such as fresh basil sprigs or lemon leaves.

8 ounces very sharp white cheddar cheese

12 ounces jarred sweet salad peppers

9 extra-large eggs

Preheat the oven to 350 degrees.

Grate the cheese on the large holes of a box grater. Spray an 8-by-8-inch pan with nonstick cooking spray. Scatter cheese evenly on bottom.

Save 3 tablespoons liquid from peppers, then drain peppers thoroughly in a colander. Pat peppers dry and distribute evenly on cheese. Put the eggs, ¾ teaspoon salt, and a liberal amount of freshly ground black pepper in bowl of an electric mixer. Beat for 2 minutes, then add reserved pepper liquid. Beat 2 minutes longer, until very light.

Pour eggs over peppers and bake for 30 minutes, until just set. Let cool and refrigerate until firm. When ready to serve, cut into 16 squares and let come to room temperature.

MAKES 16

smoked salmon in pillows

These lovely little puffs mimic those pigs-in-blankets we all love despite their inelegance. These, however, are quite elegant and taste especially suave with a glass of bubbly.

Thaw puff pastry until pliable but still cold. Preheat the oven to 400 degrees. Roll out pastry so that it stretches to 10 by 10 inches. Cut into 20 squarish shapes that are 2½ by 2 inches.

Place 1 teaspoon cheese on bottom half of one square. Tear off a piece of salmon to fit on top. Be careful not to use too much, since the entire filling must be contained. Fold top of pastry over filling to make a neat rectangular shape. Using the tines of a fork, press down tightly on the three open sides to make a little pillow shape. Repeat with the remaining pastry squares.

Place on a baking sheet and bake for 20 to 25 minutes, until puffed and golden brown. Serve immediately.

MAKES 20

1 sheet frozen puff pastry, about 8¾ ounces

5½ ounces Boursin cheese

4 ounces good-quality smoked salmon, sliced

cherry tomato bonbons

Cherry tomatoes become instantly festive when presented in fancy little fluted paper cups generally reserved for candy and available at specialty baking stores. Guests will delight in these one-bite, pop-in-your-mouth savories. They can be filled with almost anything: prepared guacamole topped with chopped cilantro, herring in cream sauce pureed with fresh dill, store-bought hummus with a chiffonade of basil, cooked lentils whipped up with black olive tapenade, whitefish salad mixed with truffle oil, lobster salad scattered with minced chives, or the following:

32 to 36 medium cherry tomatoes

2 ounces anchovies with capers in oil

8 ounces cream cheese, softened

Wash the tomatoes and remove any stems. Using a very sharp knife, slice off the top third (opposite the stem end) of each tomato. You can use these pieces to top each filled tomato. With a small spoon, scoop out and discard the insides of the tomatoes. Sprinkle the insides lightly with salt and turn upside down on a paper towel to drain.

Drain anchovies, reserving ½ teaspoon of the oil. Finely chop anchovies and capers. Put cream cheese in a shallow bowl. Mash with a fork. Add anchovies and capers, reserved oil, and a grinding of black pepper. Mash until thoroughly incorporated. Chill.

Turn tomatoes right side up and fill them, mounding on top. Chill until ready to serve. Place each tomato in a decorative 1-inch fluted paper cup. Top with one of the reserved tomato pieces or leave as is. Serve on a platter.

MAKES 32 TO 36

hot and crispy cheese truffles

If one hors d'oeuvre can elicit immediate holiday cheer, then this is it, especially if you serve these lacy morsels of golden, molten cheese with a glass of sparkling cider. Looking much more difficult to make than they are, the secret is real French Gruyère, or Comté, or authentic Swiss Emmental cheese held together by white "polenta." I use grapeseed oil because it gets quite hot without smoking, but peanut oil or vegetable oil will suffice. Serve on a plate lined with a big white linen napkin. Garnish with curly parsley for old time's sake, or lacy chervil, if available.

1 pound French Gruyère, Comté, or Swiss Emmental

3 cups white cornmeal

Grapeseed, peanut, or vegetable oil, for frying

Grate cheese on large holes of a box grater and set aside.

In a large saucepan, bring 2½ cups water and 1 heaping teaspoon salt to a boil. Gradually stir in 2 cups cornmeal, letting cornmeal fall through your fingers into the pan. Whisking constantly, cook over medium heat for 4 to 5 minutes. When ready, the mixture should come away from the sides of the pan. Remove from heat and stir in cheese. Add a generous amount of freshly ground black pepper and stir until thoroughly incorporated.

When cool, roll mixture into ½-inch balls, then roll balls in remaining cornmeal to coat.

Pour 2 inches oil into a medium pot. Heat oil to 375 degrees. Add balls in batches and cook for 2 to 3 minutes, until golden brown. Drain on paper towels. Sprinkle with salt and serve immediately.

MAKES ABOUT 72

a few quick and easy hors d'oeuvres

golden almonds with dill

2 cups whole shelled almonds with skins, about 10 ounces

¼ cup garlic oil

1 bunch fresh dill

Put almonds in a saucepan and cover with water. Bring to a boil. Boil for 30 seconds only and immediately drain in a colander. Slip almonds from their skins and pat dry. (You can also used blanched almonds.) Heat oil in a large nonstick skillet, add almonds, and sauté over medium-high heat for 1 minute. Finely chop ¼ cup dill and add to pan. Cook for several minutes, stirring constantly, until almonds are golden and dill is crisp. Add salt and pepper to taste. Drain on paper towels. Garnish with chopped dill.

MAKES 2 CUPS

stuffed olives in sweet vermouth

10 ounces super colossal stuffed olives

3 large cloves garlic

1½ to 2 cups sweet vermouth

Drain olives in a colander. Wash well under cold water and pat dry. Place in a jar with a lid. Peel garlic and slice lengthwise into paper-thin slices. Add to olives. Pour in vermouth to cover. Place lid on the jar and shake. Refrigerate for 4 to 6 hours.

MAKES ABOUT 32

fried chickpeas with walnut oil and sage

Pat chickpeas dry, whether using canned or freshly cooked. Heat oil in a large nonstick skillet. Add chickpeas and fry until crisp and golden brown. Add crumbled sage leaves, ½ teaspoon salt, and freshly ground black pepper to taste. Continue to cook for 2 minutes. Drizzle with a little more oil if chickpeas look dry. Serve warm in a shallow bowl.

MAKES 3 CUPS

*You can find whole dried sage leaves in many Middle Eastern markets, specialty food stores, or spice stores.

3 cups cooked chickpeas

4½ tablespoons walnut oil

3 tablespoons whole dried sage leaves, crumbled *

peppery pecans

Preheat the oven to 350 degrees. In a large nonstick skillet, melt butter and add 2 table-spoons Worcestershire sauce and lots of freshly ground black pepper. Add pecans and a large pinch of salt. Stir and cook over medium heat for 3 minutes, making sure the nuts are coated. Transfer to a baking sheet and bake for 12 minutes, stirring often. Drain on paper towels. Toss with more salt, pepper, and remaining Worcestershire sauce.

MAKES ABOUT 4 CUPS

4 tablespoons unsalted butter

3 tablespoons Worcestershire sauce

4 cups shelled pecan halves, about 16 ounces

tomato-anisette "demitasse"

½ cup heavy cream

3 cups Bloody Mary mix

3 tablespoons anisette

In a small bowl, whip cream and a pinch of salt until thick. In a small saucepan, bring Bloody Mary mix (available in most supermarkets) just to a boil. Lower heat and simmer for 1 minute. Put 1 teaspoon anisette into 6 or 8 warmed demitasse cups. Barely fill with hot Bloody Mary mix and top with whipped cream. Serve immediately.

MAKES 6 TO 8

tiny oysters with champagne mignonette

¾ cup champagne vinegar

4 large shallots

36 small oysters

In a small bowl, mix vinegar, ½ cup cold water, and 2 teaspoons mignonette (coarsely ground) black pepper. (It can be purchased this way.) Peel shallots and finely mince to get 6 tablespoons. Add to vinegar mixture. Let sit for 1 hour to soften shallots. Open the oysters or have your fish store do it, leaving the oysters in their shells. Arrange oysters on rock salt, crushed ice, or blanched seaweed. Serve with mignonette sauce for dipping.

SERVES 6

quesadillas with fontina and truffle oil

Preheat the oven to 300 degrees. Place 4 tortillas on a flat surface. Grate cheese on large holes of a box grater. Distribute cheese evenly on tortillas. Drizzle with truffle oil. Add salt and coarsely ground black pepper. Cover each with a tortilla and press down tightly. Brush a large nonstick skillet with a little truffle oil. Add 1 quesadilla and cook over medium-high heat for 2 to 3 minutes on each side until golden, pressing down with a spatula. Repeat with remaining quesadillas. Place on a baking sheet and keep warm in oven until ready to serve. Cut into wedges.

MAKES 24 PIECES

8 (8-inch) flour tortillas

12 ounces Italian fontina cheese

3 or more tablespoons white truffle oil

foie gras "kisses"

Place prunes in a bowl. Add liqueur and 1 cup boiling water. Let sit for 20 minutes. Drain prunes, reserving liquid. Pat dry. Stuff prunes with pâté, mounding on top. If desired, put a thin slice of any remaining prunes on top to create little sandwiches. Place reserved liquid in a saucepan and cook until reduced to ¼ cup. Glaze prunes with liquid, using a pastry brush. Let cool.

MAKES 24

24 extra-large pitted prunes

1 cup B&B or Grand Marnier

8 ounces pâté de fole gras

soups and starters

Shell-Roasted Oysters,
Black Caviar Pearls

Butternut Squash Soup with Leek Cream

Sweet Garlic-Fennel Bisque

Double Chicken Consommé
with Sherry

Christmas Gravlax, Sweet Mustard Sauce

Santa Claus Melon with Prosciutto

Salad of Fancy Greens
and Roasted Clementines

Sausages "al Vino"
with Red and Green Grapes

Slow-Roasted Tomato and Watercress Salad

shell-roasted oysters, black caviar pearls

Roasting oysters in their shells sure beats prying them open. With a blast of heat they reveal themselves, slowly and dramatically. Add your own pearls—the best caviar, and as much of it as you can afford.

Preheat the oven to 500 degrees. Wash oysters thoroughly. Place on a baking sheet and roast for 15 minutes, or until shells begin to open.

Meanwhile, melt butter in a small saucepan. Do not let brown.

When oysters open, open them as wide as possible with a small knife without detaching top shell from bottom. Drizzle each with hot butter and add a dollop of caviar. Scatter very coarse salt and blanched seaweed or lemon leaves on 6 large plates. Place 6 oysters on each plate. Serve immediately.

SERVES 6

36 large oysters, unopened in shells

6 tablespoons unsalted butter

1/3 cup black caviar, sevruga or beluga

NICE TOUCH
Cut small lemons
in half and wrap
each half in
cheesecloth tied
with a ribbon.
Pile in a small bowl
and let guests
help themselves.

butternut squash soup with leek cream

When roasted and caramelized, butternut squash produces a luxuriously flavored soup. Leeks flavor the broth and also are transformed into a pale jade cream that is swirled into a pool of bright orange. For an extra flourish, cut the dark green parts of the leeks into diamond shapes, blanch them quickly, and scatter on the hot soup.

2 butternut squash, 3 pounds total

1½ pounds medium leeks

1¾ cups heavy cream

Preheat the oven to 400 degrees. Cut squash in half lengthwise. Discard seeds and any stringy fibers. Cut in half again across the width. Place squash, cut side down, on a baking sheet. Pour in ⅓ cup water. Bake for 1 hour, or until flesh is soft and caramelized.

Meanwhile, wash leeks well. Cut off all green parts except 1 inch of pale green. Slice white and pale green parts into thin rounds and place in a medium pot with 3½ cups water, 1 cup cream, and 4 teaspoons salt. Bring to a boil. Cover and simmer for 30 minutes.

Scoop flesh from cooked squash and add to pot. Cook over medium heat for 15 minutes. Transfer to a food processor in several batches. Process until very smooth. Return to pot.

To make leek cream: Put remaining ¾ cup cream and ¼ cup water in a small saucepan. Finely chop 1 cup leek greens. Add to cream. Simmer for 20 minutes, until soft but still green. Transfer to a blender and puree until thick and very smooth. Add salt to taste.

When ready to serve, reheat soup and adjust seasoning. Garnish with a little leek cream and additional blanched leeks, if desired.

SERVES 8

sweet garlic-fennel bisque

A profusion of garlic cloves and fennel sweeten in long-simmering cream to become a wondrous soup that can be made early in the day and reheated. Freshly chopped fennel fronds give it a brighter anise flavor. It might rival oyster bisque as a new holiday favorite.

3 large heads of garlic, about 4 ounces

2 cups heavy cream

2 large fennel bulbs, about 1 pound each

Peel garlic and place in a medium pot. Add cream and bring just to a boil. Lower heat, cover, and simmer for 40 minutes, or until garlic is very soft.

Meanwhile, remove wispy fronds from fennel, wrap in wet paper towels, and refrigerate. Cut fennel bulbs into ½-inch pieces, removing any brown spots. Place in a colander and wash well. Drain.

After 40 minutes, add fennel and 3 cups water to hot garlic cream. Bring just to a boil, then lower heat. Cover and simmer for 40 minutes, or until fennel is very soft.

Transfer contents to a blender or food processor. Puree in several batches until very, very smooth. Return to pot and add 1 teaspoon salt and finely ground white pepper to taste. Heat for several minutes, until soup thickens a bit.

Finely chop reserved fennel fronds and scatter on soup.

SERVES 6

double chicken consommé with sherry

This elemental soup with distinctive flavors is both a sophisticated way to begin a holiday meal and a lovely intermezzo served in demitasse cups. As a bonus, it is a palliative that is sure to cure any winter sniffles.

6 pounds chicken wings

2 bunches scallions

¼ cup dry sherry

Place chicken wings in a large pot with cold water to just cover. Add 1 tablespoon kosher salt and 1 teaspoon black peppercorns. Finely chop white and green parts of scallions to get 1 cup, reserving several scallions. Add chopped scallions to pot and bring to a boil. Lower heat and cover pot. Cook for 1½ hours.

Strain soup through a fine-mesh sieve into a clean pot. Save chicken wings. Continue to cook soup until reduced to 8 cups. Skim as much fat as possible from surface. Add sherry and several scallions, very thinly sliced on the bias. Cook for several minutes, until very hot. Add salt, pepper, or sherry to taste.

Remove meat from warm chicken wings. Mound warm chicken in each of 8 shallow soup plates. Pour hot consommé over chicken.

SERVES 8

christmas gravlax, sweet mustard sauce

On any Swedish smorgasbord, once known as "the vodka table," one invariably finds gravlax—a silken preparation of raw salmon cured with dill, sugar, salt, and pepper. Once you've mastered the art of making your own, you'll never buy it again. Do as the Swedes do and garnish with crisped salmon skin. Serve with the sprightly 1-2-3 mustard sauce below and with, naturally, vodka: chill the bottle in your freezer and the vodka will become slightly viscous.

Remove all the small bones from the salmon with tweezers. Pat the fish dry. Cover the surface of fish with a mixture of ¼ cup kosher salt, 1 tablespoon butcher-grind black pepper, and the sugar. Chop enough dill to get 1½ packed cups. Save remaining dill for garnish. Cover top of fish with chopped dill. Wrap tightly in plastic wrap. Weight down with several bricks or cans or jars filled with water. Refrigerate for 24 to 48 hours, pouring off any liquid once or twice during curing process. Before serving, scrape off most of dill and seasonings and slice thinly on the bias into ⅛-inch slices. Arrange on a large platter and wrap until ready to serve.

Cut the skin across the width into 12 strips. Heat a large cast-iron skillet and cook the strips of skin until lightly browned, about 1 minute on each side. Drain on paper towels. Roll each strip around a small clump of dill and place on its flat side so that dill fronds stick straight up. Garnish platter with the rolls.

SERVES 12

3-pound side of salmon, cut from the center, skin on

¼ cup sugar

2 large bunches dill

SWEET MUSTARD SAUCE

In a small bowl, put 6 tablespoons sugar and ¼ cup distilled white vinegar. Stir until dissolved. Whisk in ½ cup Dijon mustard until thick. Cover and refrigerate 24 hours. Makes 1 cup and lasts for a month in the refrigerator.

santa claus melon with prosciutto

My version of this classic is "spiked" for the holidays and makes use of a melon with an irresistible name. Also known as Christmas melon, it has a long oval shape and pale green flesh similar to honeydew. Slender jade arcs marinate in a puddle of white port then are draped with the best imported prosciutto money can buy.

1 large ripe Santa Claus melon

2 cups white port

12 ounces imported prosciutto di Parma or San Daniele, thinly sliced

Cut melon in half and remove seeds. Cut each half into ¼-inch-thick wedges and remove skin with a sharp knife. Place melon in a shallow casserole. Pour port over melon. Cover and refrigerate for up to 3 hours.

Bring prosciutto to room temperature. Drain melon well and place in overlapping pattern on each of 6 large plates. Drape with overlapping slices of prosciutto. Scatter with coarsely ground black pepper. Serve immediately.

As a garnish, you can make small balls from remaining melon, using a tiny melon baller. Scatter around prosciutto.

SERVES 6

salad of fancy greens and roasted clementines

Aren't we lucky that tucked right next to the iceberg lettuce in every supermarket are packages of organic mixed fancy greens? With no effort at all a glorious salad can be had. Roasted clementines look like ornaments sitting in the center of a field of greens and add great body to the creamy citrus dressing.

14 clementines

⅔ cup olive oil

8 ounces mesclun or mixed organic greens

Preheat the broiler. Cut 4 clementines in half through the equator and place, cut side up, in a pie pan. Brush with a little oil and broil for several minutes, until slightly blackened and soft. Remove from broiler and set aside.

Peel 6 clementines, cut into ¼ inch thick slices, and set aside.

Squeeze the remaining clementines to get ½ cup juice. Add to blender with ½ cup oil and one broiled clementine half. Add the juice of another broiled clementine half. Process until dressing is thick and creamy, adding salt and pepper to taste.

Toss mesclun with a little of the remaining oil and add salt to taste. Place on each of 6 large plates. Place a broiled clementine half in center of each and surround with sliced clementines. Drizzle dressing lightly over the greens. Serve immediately.

SERVES 6

sausages "al vino" with red and green grapes

Sausages with green grapes is a country dish from the region of Umbria in Italy. I added red grapes for holiday cheer. The juice from both grapes offers a slightly sweet and acidic counterpoint to the sausages. Dry red wine supplies a special complexity. Roasted grapes add an extra burst of sweetness and intensity. Serve atop a bed of Olive Oil Mashed Potatoes (page 56) for an exceptional first course. Or double the portion and call it dinner.

2½ pounds seedless grapes (half red, half green)

8 Italian sausages, about 2 pounds (sweet and hot)

1 cup dry red wine

Make roasted grapes: Preheat the oven to 275 degrees. Wash grapes and remove stems. Place 1 cup of each color grapes on a baking sheet and bake for 1 hour and 30 minutes, shaking the pan often, until grapes shrivel and caramelize. This can be done in advance.

Place 1 cup of each color fresh grapes in a food processor and process thoroughly. Pour contents through a coarse-mesh sieve to extract juice; discard solids in the sieve. You should have 1 cup juice.

Prick sausages all over with a fork. Place in a large nonstick skillet and cook over medium-high heat until browned all over and almost cooked through. Add grape juice and cook for a few minutes. Add remaining fresh grapes and cook until grapes have softened but not collapsed. Using a slotted spoon, transfer sausages and grapes to a platter. Keep warm. Raise heat to high and add wine. Cook until sauce has thickened substantially, about 5 minutes, and pour over sausages and grapes. Scatter roasted grapes on top. Serve hot.

SERVES 8

slow-roasted tomato and watercress salad

This salad sports the colors of the season—fleshy tomatoes against a background of crisp greenery. Slow-roasting tomatoes intensifies their flavor—which is a good thing this time of year. Soft and yielding, they are whirled into a creamy, voluptuous dressing.

Preheat the oven to 275 degrees.

Wash tomatoes and pat dry. Cut 15 of the tomatoes in half lengthwise and place, cut side up, on a baking sheet. Drizzle with 1 tablespoon oil and sprinkle with salt and pepper. Bake for 2½ hours, carefully turning several times during baking. You want the tomatoes to retain their shape. Remove from oven and let cool.

Put 12 roasted tomato halves in a blender. Add 6 tablespoons oil and up to ¾ cup water and process to make a smooth, thick, but pourable dressing. Add salt and pepper to taste.

Wash watercress and dry well. Discard thick stems. Place watercress in a bowl and toss with 1 tablespoon oil and a pinch of salt. Arrange mounds of watercress on 6 large plates. Top each with 3 roasted tomato halves. Slice remaining tomato very thin and surround each mound with 3 slices as a garnish. Pour dressing over salads. Serve immediately.

SERVES 6

16 large ripe plum (Roma) tomatoes

½ cup garlic oil

3 large bunches watercress

main courses

Three-Minute Wasabi Salmon

Salmon Baked in a Golden Balloon

"Three French Hens"

Pistachio-Crusted Chilean Sea Bass

Sage-Roasted Capon with Wild Mushrooms

Crisped Duck with Turnips, Port Reduction

"Pomander" Turkey
with Clove-Studded Oranges

Roast Goose with Chestnuts and Prunes

Glazed Christmas Ham

Prime Ribs of Beef, Cabernet-Garlic "Jus"

Rib-Eye Roast in the Style of Gravlax

Bay-Smoked Châteaubriand with Marsala

three-minute wasabi salmon

Three minutes refers to the amount of time it takes to prep the salmon. You will be amazed at the texture and flavor of this unusual dish. Wasabi, often referred to as Japanese horseradish, is spunky and versatile and thankfully available in most supermarkets. This dish is truly more than the sum of its parts and terrific for company. It looks especially beautiful surrounded by kumquats with their leaves.

Preheat the oven to 450 degrees.

With tweezers, remove any little bones from fish. Season fish with salt and pepper.

Mix wasabi with 5 to 6 tablespoons water to form a smooth, thick paste. Stir into mayonnaise and mix thoroughly. Add a pinch of salt and freshly ground white pepper. Spread mixture on fish to cover completely.

Place on a baking sheet and bake for 20 minutes. Do not overcook; fish should be moist. It may take a few minutes more or less, depending on thickness of fish. The top of the fish should be slightly golden. Serve immediately.

SERVES 8

3½- to 4-pound side of salmon, skin on

6 tablespoons wasabi powder

1½ cups mayonnaise

salmon baked in a golden balloon

The magic of this dish is its presentation. Paper-thin slices of green-edged zucchini form the "scales" on an entire side of coral-hued salmon. The whole thing is wrapped in an expanse of gold foil to make a seal-tight pouch. This method of cooking, known as en papillote, is generally prepared with parchment paper and produces incredibly moist flesh and flavorful juices. Fabulous vapors escape when the packet is slashed open. Because of its hefty weight, it is better to bake the fish in a sturdier material, and gold foil makes it look like a gift. Gold foil is available in many specialty baking stores, but 18-inch heavy-duty aluminum foil can be substituted. The amazing sauce is made in the style of a classic French butter sauce, beurre blanc.

3-pound side of salmon, skin removed

2½ pounds medium zucchini

8 tablespoons unsalted butter

Preheat the oven to 450 degrees.

Using tweezers, remove any little bones from fish. Season fish with salt and pepper. Slice 2 or 3 zucchini into paper-thin rounds. Place in a tight overlapping fashion on top side of fish to resemble scales, being sure to completely cover fish. (You can do this early in the day; wrap tightly in plastic wrap and refrigerate.)

Tear off a piece of foil that is 2½ times the length of the fish. Place fish on foil. Melt 4 tablespoons butter and pour over fish. Season with salt and pepper. Fold foil over fish and crimp the edges, tightly rolling a 2-inch airtight seal. Place on a baking sheet.

Roast for 40 minutes. The package will puff up like a balloon.

Meanwhile, prepare sauce: Cut the remaining zucchini, about 1 pound, into 1-inch chunks. Place in a saucepan with ½ cup cold water and ¼ teaspoon salt. Bring to a boil. Cover pan and simmer for 15 to 20 minutes, or until zucchini is very soft, but still green. Transfer contents to a blender (being careful to let some steam escape from top of blender) and process until very smooth. Cut remaining butter into small pieces and add to blender. Process until thick and creamy. Return sauce to saucepan. (If sauce gets too thick, add more water.)

When fish is cooked, immediately transfer "balloon" to a platter and present to your guests. Slash open package. Cut fish into portions and remove with a spatula. Be sure to pour any juices over fish. Gently heat sauce and serve with fish.

SERVES 6

"three french hens"

Soaking these small birds in brine keeps them particularly moist. Roasting them on a bed of piney rosemary makes your whole house smell like Christmas should. For fun, and a decidedly French look, buy those little ruffled papers to put on the legs of the hens (generally used for lamb chops).

3 Cornish hens, 1½ pounds each

12 ounces pancetta, cut into ¼-inch-thick slices

4 large bunches rosemary

Remove giblets and set aside. Place hens in a very large bowl and cover with cold water. Add 1 cup kosher salt and stir until salt dissolves. Refrigerate for 6 to 8 hours.

Preheat the oven to 375 degrees.

Remove hens from brine and pat dry. Cut pancetta into small cubes. Add 2 tablespoons finely minced rosemary and lots of coarsely ground black pepper. Place pancetta mixture in a large nonstick skillet and cook over medium heat for about 5 minutes, until pancetta is beginning to crisp and some of the fat is rendered. Stuff the birds with this mixture. Brush rendered fat on hens. Truss with string, securing a long branch of rosemary on top of each bird.

Spread 1 bunch of rosemary in a shallow roasting pan. Place hens on rosemary. Bake for 40 minutes. Place under broiler for 1 to 2 minutes to brown.

Meanwhile, discard liver and place giblets in a saucepan. Add 2½ cups cold water and 2 large sprigs rosemary. Bring to a boil. Lower heat and simmer for 30 minutes. Strain through a fine-mesh sieve into a clean saucepan and cook until stock is reduced to 1 cup.

Transfer hens and rosemary to a cutting board. Add stock to pan and scrape up any browned bits. Strain again through sieve into saucepan and cook over high heat until sauce is syrupy. Cut hens in half and place on a serving platter. Pour hot sauce over hens and garnish with remaining rosemary.

SERVES 6

pistachio-crusted chilean sea bass

There are few better fish dishes grand enough to rival time-honored holiday entrees. Nestled under a pale green crust, this thick juicy fish satisfies the desire for something special and is sure to please any meat eaters you have around your table. It makes a dramatic entrance on a large white platter decorated with boughs of holly. Tra lu la.

3½-pound Chilean sea bass fillet, cut from the center

1¼ cups shelled unsalted pistachios

1¼ cups best-quality prepared pesto

Preheat the oven to 400 degrees.

Using tweezers, remove any bones running down center of fish. Line a baking sheet with parchment paper or foil. Place fish on sheet and sprinkle both sides with salt.

Process pistachios in bowl of a food processor until coarsely ground. Do not overprocess; you want small, discernible pieces, not powder.

Spread pesto thickly on top of fish to coat completely, draining most of the oil from the pesto as you go. Dust pesto with freshly ground black pepper. Pack pistachios on pesto to cover evenly and press down lightly to obtain a thick nut crust.

Bake for 35 to 40 minutes, or until desired doneness. Do not overcook; it is important to keep the fish moist and juicy. Remove from oven. Transfer fish to a large warm platter. Add a little boiling water to the bottom of the pan to scrape up any pan juices. Strain quickly through a fine-mesh sieve and pour over fish. Serve immediately.

SERVES 8

sage-roasted capon with wild mushrooms

Fresh sage leaves are placed under the skin of this plump bird for a dramatic look. This is a riff on a preparation known as demi-deuil *or "half-mourning," in which slices of black truffles are placed under the skin of a chicken. This version is particularly celebratory, even without the truffles, because of its profusion of woodsy mushrooms. Use dried porcini mushrooms for the most rewarding flavor.*

8- to 9-pound capon

4 large bunches sage

1½ cups dried mushrooms

Preheat the oven to 375 degrees.

Wash capon and pat dry. Discard giblets or save for another use. Remove fat lobes near opening of cavity and melt in a small skillet over low heat.

Using your finger, carefully separate the breast skin from the flesh of the capon. Slip large sage leaves under skin to cover as much surface as possible. Leaves should lie flat under the skin. Save 8 large sage leaves for later and place 1 whole bunch sage in cavity. Truss with string, tying legs together, and place in a shallow roasting pan. Pour melted fat over capon and season with salt and pepper.

Place ⅓ cup dried mushrooms in a spice/coffee grinder or in a blender and process to a powder. Sprinkle capon with mushroom powder. Roast for 1 hour and 45 minutes, basting halfway through cooking time.

Place remaining mushrooms in a bowl. Pour 4 cups boiling water over mushrooms and soak for 1 hour. Drain in a coffee filter paper, reserving strained liquid. Wash mushrooms to remove any grit. Save mushrooms and mushroom liquid separately.

When a meat thermometer registers 165 degrees in the thick part of the thigh, remove capon from oven. Add mushroom liquid to roasting pan and scrape up any browned bits. Strain the liquid through a fine-mesh sieve into a saucepan. Add 8 sage leaves and cook over high heat until syrupy and reduced to 1½ cups. Add mushrooms, and salt and pepper to taste. Cook for several minutes.

Carve capon as desired and serve with hot mushroom sauce. Garnish with any remaining sage leaves.

SERVES 6

crisped duck with turnips, port reduction

Since most of us don't make duck regularly at home, here's a special gift for your guests. It's even getting difficult to find on most restaurant menus. My method, both simple and sublime, ensures a crisp, crackling exterior and succulent flesh. If your turnips come with leaves, do save them. They are perfect for steaming and garnishing your platter. If you're serving more people, make 2 ducks.

5-pound duck

2 pounds (about 16) small white turnips, peeled and cut in half

2 cups tawny port

Preheat the oven to 350 degrees.

Remove giblets and wing tips from duck and set aside. Discard liver (or sauté it as a little gift for yourself!). Put giblets and wing tips in a medium saucepan with water to cover. Add ½ teaspoon salt and 10 black peppercorns and bring to a boil. Lower heat and simmer for 1 hour. Strain through a fine-mesh sieve into a clean saucepan. Cook over medium heat until reduced to ½ cup. Set stock aside.

Remove lobes of fat from duck and discard. Wash duck and pat dry thoroughly. Prick skin all over with a fork. Rub salt and pepper into skin and truss duck with string.

Place duck on a rack fit into a broiler pan or shallow roasting pan. Roast for 1¼ hours. Remove duck from rack and pour off fat. Place duck directly in broiler pan and surround with turnips. Return to oven and roast for 25 minutes longer. Turn turnips over and cook for an additional 20 minutes. Raise oven temperature to 500 degrees and cook for 15 minutes longer. Total roasting time will be 2 hours and 15 minutes.

While duck is cooking, put ½ cup reduced duck stock in a saucepan with 1 cup port. Bring to a boil and cook over medium heat until reduced to ½ cup, about 15 minutes. In another saucepan, cook remaining port over medium heat until reduced to ¼ cup. Add to reduced duck stock–port mixture. Add salt and freshly ground black pepper to taste.

Remove duck and turnips from oven. Cut duck into quarters and serve with turnips and port reduction.

SERVES 4

"pomander" turkey with clove-studded oranges

This succulent bird gets its moist texture from quick brining and slow roasting. Its delicate fragrance and flavor come from stuffing the bird with festive pomanders—juicy oranges studded with whole cloves that are often used for decoration.

14-pound turkey

4 large oranges

2 tablespoons whole cloves

Wash turkey and remove giblets (discard liver; reserve remaining giblets). Place turkey in a pot large enough to fit comfortably, with cold water to cover. Add 1 cup kosher salt and stir to dissolve. Cover and let sit for 2 hours at room temperature, turning several times.

Preheat the oven to 350 degrees.

Remove turkey from brine. Pat dry. Wash 2 oranges and stud them with 40 cloves per orange, ½ inch apart, as if you were inserting thumbtacks. Place these pomanders in cavity of turkey, then truss with string to secure wings and hold legs together. Season with freshly ground black pepper. Cover breast tightly with foil. Roast for 2 hours.

Meanwhile, place reserved giblets in a saucepan. Add 4 cups water to cover. Add ½ tablespoon cloves. Bring to a boil. Skim any foam off the surface, lower heat to medium, and simmer for 30 minutes. Strain through a fine-mesh sieve and return to pan. Cook again until reduced to 4 cups. Set aside.

After 4 hours, remove foil from turkey breast and raise temperature to 400 degrees. Cook turkey for about 30 minutes longer, basting frequently with drippings. Remove when a meat thermometer registers 165 degrees in the thick part of the thigh. Transfer to a cutting board. Let rest while you prepare gravy.

Pour off fat from pan. Pour reserved stock into pan and scrape up any browned bits. Strain pan juices through a fine-mesh sieve into clean saucepan. Grate the rind of remaining 2 oranges and add to pan juices. Add the juice of the oranges and bring to a boil. Lower heat and cook until sauce is syrupy and reduced to about 1½ cups. Add salt and pepper to taste.

Remove pomanders from turkey cavity and cut them into wedges. Carve turkey as desired. Serve with pomanders, for decoration, and hot gravy.

SERVES 8 TO 10

roast goose with chestnuts and prunes

Roasting chestnuts and preparing goose are much easier than you think. This is a golden goose whose straightforward methodology came from my friend Larry Freundlich, who wrote the first beloved Blue Dog book. As a small present for yourself, sauté the liver in goose fat, sprinkle with salt and freshly grated nutmeg, then eat atop a slice of toasted brioche. Sip some Sauternes and put on an old Bing Crosby recording.

1½ pounds fresh chestnuts

1½ pounds large pitted prunes

10- to 12-pound fresh goose with giblets

Preheat the oven to 375 degrees.

Using a small sharp knife, make an X on the pointed end of each chestnut. Place in one layer on a baking sheet and roast for 40 minutes. Let cool and peel off shells.

Place prunes in a bowl. Add boiling water to cover. Let sit for 15 minutes, then drain. Mix chestnuts with half of the drained prunes. Toss with a little salt and pepper. Set aside.

Remove giblets from goose. Cut off tips and first joints of wings and set aside. Remove any large pockets of fat from goose. Cut off all but 3 inches of skin near the neck.

Stuff cavity with chestnut-prune mixture. Truss goose with string. Place goose on rack in a roasting pan. Prick skin all over with tip of small knife, being careful not to puncture flesh. Season with salt and pepper, rubbing into skin with your fingers. Roast for 2 hours.

Meanwhile, place giblets (except liver) and wing tips in a large saucepan with water to cover. Add 1 teaspoon black peppercorns and cook with cover askew for 1 hour, skimming the surface often. Add remaining prunes and cook for 1 hour longer, continuing to skim and adding water as necessary. Remove prunes and strain stock through a fine-mesh sieve; return stock to pan. Continue to cook stock until syrupy and reduced to about 3 cups.

Transfer prunes to a food mill or blender and process until very smooth. Add enough prune puree to stock to obtain a dark, thick, pourable gravy. Add salt and pepper.

After 2 hours, check goose with thermometer. Breast meat should be 165 degrees. Remove if done, or continue to cook until desired temperature is reached.

Remove goose from oven and let rest for 10 minutes. Cut off string and spoon out chestnuts and prunes. Cut off legs and thighs and carve breast into thick slices. Top with chestnuts and prunes, and serve hot prune gravy alongside.

SERVES 6

glazed christmas ham

House-filling aromas will trigger mouthwatering anticipation. A quintessential dish at Christmas, this particular ham is elemental in its flavors—salty meat, sharp mustard, sweet crust—yet it hits your palate like a harmonious chord. Simple cooking techniques keep it moist and succulent; a cinnamon-sugar coating makes it special.

10-pound smoked ready-to-cook ham, shank portion

1 cup coarse-grain mustard

1 cup cinnamon-sugar *

*You can buy cinnamon-sugar or make your own by mixing 1 cup granulated sugar with 1½ tablespoons ground cinnamon.

Preheat the oven to 325 degrees.

Place ham in a shallow roasting pan and add ⅛ inch water to pan. Cover ham with foil and bake for 15 to 16 minutes per pound, for a total of about 2 hours and 40 minutes. (Adjust cooking time if your ham is other than 10 pounds.)

After 2 hours and 15 minutes, remove ham from oven and increase temperature to 450 degrees. Pour most of fat from pan. Using a sharp, thin-bladed knife, remove the rind, except for area around shank bone, and most of the fat. Score the remaining fat by cutting diagonal slashes in a diamond pattern. Cover the surface thickly with mustard, then heavily coat with cinnamon-sugar, patting down if necessary. Add freshly ground black pepper and return to oven for 25 minutes, until sugar melts and hardens. It will become a bit crackly.

Present on a large platter, decorated as desired. Carve and serve while hot.

SERVES 12

prime ribs of beef, cabernet-garlic "jus"

Ask your butcher for the first five ribs, or a "7-inch cut," with the chine bone removed for easy carving. This is a very expensive piece of meat, but it is the most generous way I know to celebrate the holidays.

Preheat the oven to 500 degrees.

Let meat come to room temperature. This will take about 1½ hours. Peel 1 head garlic and add cloves to food processor. Process until finely minced and rub all over meat. Season meat heavily with coarse salt and freshly ground black pepper.

Place roast, rib side down, in a heavy, shallow roasting pan. Cut ¼ inch from tops of garlic heads and surround roast with them cut side down. Place meat in oven, then reduce temperature to 300 degrees. Turn garlic over after 1½ hours and cook for another 1½ hours, or until a meat thermometer registers 130 degrees for rare.

When roast is done to desired temperature, transfer roast and heads of garlic to a large cutting board. Let rest for 15 minutes while you prepare the "jus": Pour off most of the fat from pan and save. Pour in wine and 1 cup water. Cut 1 head of garlic in half and squeeze the pulp into pan. Cook over high heat about 10 minutes, scraping up browned bits. Strain into a clean saucepan and add reserved fat. Continue to cook until sauce gets a little syrupy. Season "jus" with salt and pepper.

Carve meat as desired. Add all drippings from the cutting board to the "jus" and quickly bring to a boil. Serve the beef surrounded with heads of garlic and hot "jus."

SERVES 10

5-rib standing prime rib roast, about 12 pounds

12 very large heads garlic

3 cups Cabernet Sauvignon

rib-eye roast in the style of gravlax

Gravlax is a cured salmon dish whose roots date back to medieval times in Scandinavia (see recipe on page 27). In this more unusual preparation, beef, instead, is cured for 24 hours in a mixture of fresh dill, sugar, salt, and pepper. The result is extraordinarily tender, thick, rosy slices, perfect for Santa should he come to visit.

3½-pound tied rib-eye roast, about 7 inches long and 5 inches in diameter

2 large bunches fresh dill

3 tablespoons sugar

Pat beef dry with a paper towel.

Wash dill and dry thoroughly. Finely chop enough leaves to yield 1 cup, firmly packed. Save remaining dill for garnish.

Mix sugar, ¼ cup kosher salt, and 1 teaspoon coarsely ground black pepper in a small bowl. Coat all sides of meat with this mixture, rubbing it into the surface of the roast. Pat chopped dill on top, bottom, and sides of roast. Wrap tightly in plastic wrap.

Place meat in a small roasting pan and weight down with a baking sheet topped with several heavy cans, or a teapot filled with water. Place in refrigerator and let marinate for 24 hours.

When ready to cook, remove roast from plastic wrap and let sit at room temperature for 30 minutes. Preheat the oven to 400 degrees.

Scrape all the dill and spice mixture from the roast and discard. Place meat in a shallow, heavy roasting pan. Cook for 1 hour and 15 minutes, or until a meat thermometer registers 130 degrees for rare to medium rare.

Remove from oven. Transfer meat to a cutting board and let rest for 5 minutes. Carve into ½-inch slices and garnish with remaining dill.

SERVES 8

bay-smoked châteaubriand with marsala

If true sophistication lies in restraint, then this dish is a delicious example of that simple idea. Use an aged dry Marsala, or if your taste runs in a sweeter direction, you can substitute sweet Marsala from a good producer. Marsala, a fortified wine from Sicily, has been produced for over 200 years.

Preheat the oven to 400 degrees.

Sprinkle meat with ¼ cup Marsala and season with freshly ground black pepper.

Place remaining Marsala in a medium saucepan and bring to a boil. Lower heat and simmer until reduced by half.

In the center of a heavy, shallow roasting pan, scatter 15 of the bay leaves. Place the beef on top. Tuck the remaining bay leaves on top of the beef, under the butcher's string. Roast for 30 minutes. Turn the beef over and roast for 5 minutes longer, or until the internal temperature is 125 to 130 degrees for rare (cook longer if you prefer medium rare). Remove the beef from the pan and discard the fat. Let stand for 10 minutes before carving.

Quickly heat reduced Marsala and pour into the warm roasting pan, scraping up browned bits. Strain the pan juices into a small saucepan, bring to a boil, and cook over high heat until slightly thickened and reduced, about 3 minutes. Add salt and pepper to taste.

Remove the bay leaves and string from the beef. Carve into ½-inch slices and sprinkle each lightly with salt. Drizzle with Marsala reduction and serve hot, passing the remaining sauce.

SERVES 6 TO 8

3 pounds Châteaubriand or fillet of beef, tied

1 bottle aged dry Marsala

24 fresh bay leaves *

*Use fresh bay leaves, if possible. They can be found in the produce section of many supermarkets. If not available, use long, fragrant dried bay leaves from California.

festive
side dishes

Brussels Sprouts
with Sun-Dried Cranberries

Red Cabbage with Honey and Vinegar

Sugar Snaps in Orange Butter

Sweet Potato–Ginger Puree

Frenched Beans with
Crushed Macadamia Nuts

Olive Oil Mashed Potatoes

Blasted Broccoli and Grape Tomatoes

Rutabaga Mash with Glazed Shallots

Peppery-Buttery Watercress Puree

Wild Rice with Five-Hour Onions

Ruby Beets and Beet Greens,
Walnut Oil and Balsamic Syrup

brussels sprouts with sun-dried cranberries

This ultra-simple preparation wears the season's vivid colors. The cranberries look like tiny glacéed cherries and add sweet and tart notes to the buttery little cabbages. The brussels sprouts can be parboiled early in the day and sautéed right before serving.

Trim the ends of the brussels sprouts and remove any bruised outer leaves. Bring a large pot of salted water to a boil. Add brussels sprouts and boil for 10 minutes. Transfer to a colander, rinse under cold water, and drain. Dry on paper towels.

Place cranberries in a small bowl and add boiling water to cover. Let sit for 15 minutes. Drain and pat dry. Cut brussels sprouts in half through the stem end.

Melt butter in a very large sauté pan. Add brussels sprouts and cranberries and cook over medium-high heat until brussels sprouts are tender but still green with areas of golden color. Add salt and freshly ground black pepper to taste. Serve immediately.

1¼ pounds medium brussels sprouts

1 cup sun-dried cranberries

6 tablespoons unsalted butter

SERVES 6

red cabbage with honey and vinegar

The more distinctive the honey, the better the dish. I like leatherwood honey from Australia, but you might use wild thyme, buckwheat, Tupelo, or any wildflower honey. Vinegar makes red cabbage mouthwatering and fixes its garnet color. It's a wonderful counterpoint to goose, duck, or my Rib-Eye Roast in the Style of Gravlax (page 48)—and it's fat-free.

2½ pounds red cabbage

½ cup apple cider vinegar

⅓ cup aromatic honey

Remove any dark outer leaves and the core from the cabbage. Using a sharp knife, shred into ⅛-inch slices.

Place cabbage in large nonreactive pot. Add vinegar, 2 tablespoons honey, 3 cups water, 1 teaspoon whole black peppercorns, and 2 teaspoons salt. Bring to a boil. Lower heat to medium and cover pot. Cook for 2 hours, stirring often. Remove cover and cook for 30 minutes longer.

Drain cabbage in a colander, saving all the cooking liquid. Return liquid to pot and add remaining honey. Cook over high heat until syrupy and reduced to about ¾ cup. Transfer cabbage to pot and mix well. Adjust seasonings, adding vinegar, salt, or pepper, if needed. Serve hot.

SERVES 6

sugar snaps in orange butter

These clean, green-and-citrusy flavors are simple and direct and the perfect foil for every one of my Christmas main courses. Quite versatile, wouldn't you say?

Trim the ends of the pods. Remove the strings running down the their lengths. Bring a large pot of salted water to a boil. Add the peas and cook for 4 minutes, or until tender but not too soft. They should remain bright green.

2 pounds sugar snap peas

Meanwhile, grate the rind of the oranges on medium holes of a box grater to get 2 heaping tablespoons zest. Set aside. Cut oranges in half and squeeze the juice into a small saucepan and cook until reduced by half.

2 large oranges

When the sugar snaps are cooked, drain well in a colander and pat dry. Return them to the pot and add butter, orange zest, and reduced orange juice. Heat until hot; sauce should emulsify slightly. Add salt and pepper to taste and serve immediately.

5 tablespoons unsalted butter

SERVES 6

sweet potato–ginger puree

Three ingredients never tasted so voluptuous. Sure to become a holiday tradition, they're sweet and sassy, velvety, can be made well in advance, and are, quite amazingly, fat-free. This recipe can be easily doubled, tripled . . .

2 pounds sweet potatoes

4 cups apple cider

3-inch piece fresh ginger

Scrub potatoes, but do not peel. Place in a pot with salted water to cover. Bring to a boil. Lower heat and cook for about 40 minutes, or until potatoes are soft.

While potatoes are cooking, put cider in a large nonreactive saucepan and bring to a boil. Lower heat to medium and continue to cook for about 30 minutes, until reduced to 1 cup.

Peel ginger and mince very finely so that you have ¼ cup. Set aside.

When potatoes are soft, drain in a colander and peel. Cut potatoes into chunks and place in bowl of a food processor. Add reduced cider and ginger and process until very smooth and velvety. Season with salt and just a little black pepper—the ginger is very peppery. Reheat before serving.

SERVES 4 TO 6

frenched beans with crushed macadamia nuts

You could use skinny French haricots verts instead of regular green beans, but they're quadruple the price. Instead, invest a little time and "French" your own beans by running a small knife down the length of each. Toasted crushed macadamia nuts smell a little like popcorn and transform this simple vegetable into a special one.

2 pounds string beans

6 ounces unsalted macadamia nuts

½ cup lemon olive oil

Wash beans and pat dry. Trim the ends. Using a small knife, cut in half lengthwise, following the seam. Set aside.

Chop the nuts using a large chef's knife, then crush them with the bottom of a heavy glass or bottle. You want some small, distinct pieces, and some finely ground pieces. Place nuts in a nonstick skillet and cook over medium heat, stirring constantly, until toasted and golden brown. Keep warm.

Bring a large pot of salted water to a boil. Add beans and cook for about 8 minutes, or until just tender, but still bright green. Drain immediately in a colander and dry thoroughly. (Note: You can set these beans aside for later and warm them briefly in boiling water.) Place hot beans in a warm bowl and toss with oil. Add salt and pepper to taste and scatter nuts on top. Serve immediately.

SERVES 6

olive oil mashed potatoes

A big bowl of mashed potatoes is a requisite on any holiday table and these are my fragrant favorite. A wonderful sweetness comes from the garlic that's boiled with the potatoes. Be sure to use Yukon gold for their beautiful color and creamy texture.

12 large cloves garlic, peeled

6 tablespoons extra-virgin olive oil

2 pounds Yukon Gold potatoes, peeled

In a small skillet, sauté the sliced garlic in 2 tablespoons oil over low heat until tender, about 5 minutes. Do not brown. Set aside.

Bring a large saucepan of salted water to a boil. Cook potatoes and remaining garlic until potatoes are tender, about 35 minutes. Drain, reserving 1¼ cups cooking liquid.

Cut potatoes into large chunks. Pass potatoes and boiled garlic through a potato ricer, or place in a bowl and mash with a potato masher. Add sauteéd garlic with its oil and pour in remaining oil. Mix vigorously, adding as much cooking liquid as needed to make smooth and creamy. Add salt and pepper to taste. Reheat gently before serving.

SERVES 6

blasted broccoli and grape tomatoes

This is a great way to feed a crowd and keep your cool. Roasting, or blasting, veggies at a very high temperature intensifies their flavor and natural sugars and, in this case, their vibrant Christmas colors.

Preheat the oven to 450 degrees.

Peel stalks of broccoli, then cut the stalks into ½-inch pieces. Remove florets and cut into medium pieces. Place broccoli pieces in a large bowl and add tomatoes that have been washed and dried thoroughly. Toss with oil and add salt and pepper.

Place on a large baking sheet or shallow roasting pan in one layer. Roast for 18 minutes, shaking the pan twice during baking so the vegetables don't stick. Remove from oven and sprinkle with salt. Transfer to a platter and drizzle with a little extra oil. Serve immediately.

SERVES 6

1 very large head broccoli or two smaller ones

60 smallish grape tomatoes

¼ cup extra-virgin olive oil, plus more for drizzling

rutabaga mash with glazed shallots

Rutabagas, also known as Swedes or yellow turnips, are recognizable by their brownish, waxy exterior and yellow-orange flesh. I love their sweet and nutty earthiness.

2 large rutabagas, about 4 pounds total

12 medium shallots

4 tablespoons unsalted butter

Using a small sharp knife, peel rutabagas and cut into quarters. Place in a large pot with salted water to cover. Bring to a boil. Lower heat and cook for 40 minutes, or until very soft.

Meanwhile, bring a small pot of water to a boil. Add shallots and boil for 5 minutes. Drain in a colander and peel. Heat 3 tablespoons butter in a large nonstick skillet and add shallots. Cook over low heat for 25 to 30 minutes, until soft, brown, and caramelized. Do not let shallots get too brown. Add salt and pepper to taste. Set aside, keeping them warm.

Drain rutabagas well in a colander. Cut into large chunks and process in a food processor with remaining tablespoon butter. Add salt and pepper to taste. Fold in half of shallots and place in a bowl. Top with remaining shallots. Serve immediately or reheat gently in a large covered saucepan.

SERVES 8

peppery-buttery watercress puree

Small, peppery watercress is gener-ally reserved for salads but when cooked in this fashion will rival the best creamed spinach. For drama, you could serve a whole nutmeg at the table with a little grater for each guest to use. This AstroTurf-colored side dish would be especially festive served alongside a very quick 1–2–3 recipe: tiny cherry tomatoes sautéed in garlic oil with sprigs of fresh thyme.

1½ pounds large red potatoes

8 large bunches watercress

8 tablespoons unsalted butter, cold

Peel potatoes. Cut in half lengthwise, then across into ½-inch pieces. Place in a pot with salted water to cover by several inches. Bring to a boil. Cover pot and lower heat to medium. Cook for 20 minutes, until just tender.

Wash watercress and dry. Trim 1½ inches off stems of water-cress and discard. Add watercress to potatoes after 20 minutes and cook for 10 minutes longer.

Drain potatoes and watercress in a colander and place in bowl of a food processor. Puree until thick and smooth, quickly adding small pieces of cold butter. Return to pot and add salt and a little pepper to taste. Heat gently before serving.

SERVES 6

wild rice
with five-hour
onions

This is a wild dish, actually—and one that you'll make year after year. It cooks in a very low oven, for a very long time, giving you a chance to wrap the presents or decorate your tree. It can be easily reheated in case you need your oven for another task.

12 medium onions (about 3 pounds), plus 1 cup finely chopped onion

10 tablespoons unsalted butter

1 pound wild rice

Preheat the oven to 275 degrees.

Peel whole onions and place in a large heavy casserole with a lid. Thinly slice 8 tablespoons butter and scatter over onions. Cover pot and bake for 5 hours. Onions will be golden and give off lots of juices. Set aside.

One hour before serving, wash rice and drain in a colander. Melt remaining butter in a heavy medium-large pot. Add rice and chopped onion. Stir over medium heat for 5 minutes, or until rice is a bit crisp. Slowly add 2 quarts cold water and bring to a boil. Add 2 teaspoons salt and freshly ground black pepper.

Lower heat to medium, cover, and cook for 55 minutes. Uncover pot, increase heat to high, and cook for about 20 minutes, or until rice is tender. Drain in a colander if there is excess liquid. Add salt and pepper to taste and transfer to a large warmed platter.

Reheat onions on stovetop. With a slotted spoon, place onions on rice and pour juices over. Serve immediately.

SERVES 8

ruby beets and beet greens, walnut oil and balsamic syrup

This is a splendid vegetable side dish and a good example of three-part harmony. Each note seems to augment the flavor of the others. Use walnut oil imported from France.

Preheat the oven to 400 degrees.

Remove stalks and greens from beets. Remove any roots. Lay out 2 large pieces of foil and place 6 beets on each. Wrap the foil around the beets, making a balloon shape. Fold tightly on top and place both packets on a baking sheet. Bake for 1 hour and 45 minutes, until tender. Remove from oven and keep in foil.

Meanwhile, cut greens into 1-inch pieces and wash thoroughly. Bring a large pot of salted water to a boil. Add greens and cook for 5 to 10 minutes, until tender. Drain thoroughly.

Place vinegar in a saucepan and bring to a boil. Lower heat and cook until vinegar is reduced to ¾ cup. Keep warm.

Place hot cooked greens on a large platter. Cut foil, quickly peel beets, cut them into thin wedges, and place on the greens. Drizzle reduced vinegar over warm beets and greens and drizzle with oil. Sprinkle with coarse salt and freshly ground black pepper.

SERVES 6

12 medium-large beets with greens attached

1½ cups balsamic vinegar

⅓ to ½ cup walnut oil

holiday
desserts

Candy Cane Ice Cream

Eggnog-Cup Custards

Cider-Glazed Baked Apples with Marzipan

Pineapple "au Caramel"

Bracing Ginger Ice Milk

Heavenly Chocolate Cake

Poached Strawberries
with Sweet Crème Fraîche

Slow-Baked Pears with Stilton,
Warm Honey Syrup

christmas
cookies

Snowy Shortbread

Rainbow Sugar Cookies

Toasted Almond Cookies

Tiny Macaroons

"Cookies While You Sleep"

candy cane ice cream

The beauty of this ice cream is its pink hue and bracing flavor, supplied by crushed candy canes and lots of fresh lime. The real surprise is that there isn't any dairy here because it's made with "cream" of coconut. The best news is that you don't need an ice cream maker.

15 ounces cream of coconut

2 large limes

4 ounces candy canes

Place cream of coconut in a large bowl. Whisk until smooth and then whisk in 1¼ cups cold water. Grate the rind of limes to get 2 tablespoons zest and add to bowl. Cut limes in half, squeeze to get ½ cup juice, and add the juice to bowl. Whisk thoroughly.

Place in a shallow dish—a 9-inch cake pan or pie pan is good. Place in freezer for 1½ hours, whisking every 30 minutes during freezing. Break candy canes into pieces and add to bowl of a food processor. Process until finely ground but not a powder. You should have about ½ cup. Set 3 tablespoons aside and stir the rest into the half-frozen ice cream. Continue to freeze until solid, whisking periodically, about another 1½ hours.

Serve small scoops of ice cream, one on top of the other, in tall champagne flutes. Sprinkle with remaining crushed candy.

SERVES 6

eggnog-cup custards

This is new and nostalgic all at once. The technique is almost the same as for making crème caramel, but the flavor is more season-appropriate. For drama you can make one large flan and present it on a large platter garnished with holly and garlands of cranberries.

1 cup sugar

3½ cups prepared eggnog *

4 extra-large eggs, plus 2 egg yolks

*Use a commercially prepared eggnog, generally found on supermarket shelves.

Preheat the oven to 350 degrees.

Put ⅞ cup sugar in a large nonstick skillet and cook over high heat. Stir with a wooden spoon until sugar melts into a dark brown syrup with no lumps. Immediately pour sugar into 6 custard cups and let harden.

Put eggnog in a medium saucepan and bring just to a boil. Lower heat and simmer for 1 minute. Place eggs and egg yolks in bowl of an electric mixer with remaining 2 tablespoons sugar. Beat until thickened, and slowly add scalded eggnog while mixing gently, just until blended. Ladle the mixture into custard cups.

Place cups in a deep pan and carefully pour boiling water into pan to come two-thirds of the way up sides of cups. Bake for 40 minutes, or until just firm. Remove cups from water bath. Let cool. Cover with plastic wrap and chill for several hours.

Using a butter knife, carefully cut around edge of each custard to loosen. Turn over in centers of 6 dessert plates. Caramel will flow onto plate.

SERVES 6

cider-glazed baked apples with marzipan

Marzipan fills the heart of jumbo apples and then swells a bit to form a golden brown coverlet. Apple cider is reduced to a syrupy caramel sauce. Best served warm from the oven when the marzipan is soft and yielding.

Preheat the oven to 375 degrees.

Wash apples, but do not peel. Remove cores, making a hole that is 1 inch in diameter and 1½ inches deep. Remove about ¼ inch of skin around the hole. Fill holes with marzipan, about 2 tablespoons each, packing in well and spreading over apple in a smooth thin layer to cover top, especially any exposed apple flesh.

Place apples in pan large enough to hold them with some space in-between. Pour 2 cups cider over apples. Bake for 40 minutes, basting often with cider. Place under broiler briefly until just golden. When soft, transfer apples with a slotted spoon to each of 4 flat soup plates.

Meanwhile, place remaining 2 cups cider in a small saucepan and bring to a boil. Lower heat and simmer until reduced to ¾ cup.

While apples are cooling, place cider from baking pan in the saucepan with reduced cider and bring to a rapid boil. Cook over high heat until reduced to a thick syrup, about 1⅓ cups. Pour over each apple and serve warm.

4 large Rome apples, about 10 ounces each

4 ounces marzipan

1 quart fresh apple cider

SERVES 4

pineapple "au caramel"

It's fascinating how the same ingredients—heavy cream and sugar—can be combined with very different results: a dark caramel sauce and a fluff of sweet white cream. The large disk of poached golden pineapple imitates a cake that gets "iced" with whipped cream and oodles of caramel.

1 large ripe pineapple

1½ cups sugar

1¾ cups heavy cream

Cut the rind from pineapple and discard. Cut pineapple into 6 thick circles. Place in a large saucepan with water just to cover. Add ½ cup plus 2 tablespoons sugar. Bring to a boil. Lower heat and cook, covered, for 25 to 30 minutes, until soft. Let cool in syrup, then refrigerate until very cold.

Place ¼ cup water and ¾ cup sugar in a medium saucepan. Cook over medium heat until sugar dissolves and liquid is clear. Increase heat to high and cook until syrup turns a dark amber color, stirring often. Lower heat and cook for 2 minutes. Remove from heat. Carefully add 1 cup heavy cream (the mixture will bubble up and harden). Cook again over medium heat until sugar melts and mixture thickens. Continue to cook until reduced to a bit more than 1 cup. Let caramel cool to room temperature.

When ready to serve, remove pineapple from syrup with a slotted spoon. Reduce syrup until it is dark amber and thickened. Place each pineapple slice on large plate. Whip remaining ¾ cup cream with 2 tablespoons sugar until thick. Put large dollops of whipped cream on pineapple to cover and drizzle heavily with caramel, drizzling some on the plate. Pour a little reduced syrup around the pineapple. Serve immediately.

SERVES 6

bracing ginger ice milk

This simple mixture, made with buttermilk and ginger preserves, freezes beautifully and definitely lives up to its name.

Put buttermilk in a bowl. Place sugar and ²/₃ cup water in a saucepan and bring to a boil. Lower heat and cook for several minutes, until liquid is clear. Add preserves and bring to a boil. Lower heat and simmer for 1 minute. Let cool for 5 minutes, then whisk mixture into buttermilk. Whisk until smooth, then refrigerate, preferably overnight, until mixture is very cold.

Freeze in an ice cream maker following the manufacturer's directions.

SERVES 4

3 cups buttermilk, chilled

²/₃ cup sugar

²/₃ cup ginger preserves

heavenly chocolate cake

This style of cake generates names like Chocolate Decadence, Nemesis, and Obsession. I think it's heavenly, especially when it's warm and freshly baked, and it borders on celestial when served with a scoop of Candy Cane Ice Cream (page 63).

1 pound best-quality milk chocolate

10 tablespoons unsalted butter

5 extra-large eggs, at room temperature

Preheat the oven to 375 degrees.

Line a 9-inch springform pan with a round of parchment paper or aluminum foil. Spray sides of pan including parchment or foil with nonstick cooking spray.

Chop chocolate into pieces and cut butter into small chunks. Place butter and chocolate in top of a double boiler or in a bowl over simmering water. Melt, stirring frequently, until smooth. Keep warm.

In a warmed bowl, using an electric mixer, whip eggs together with a pinch of salt until mixture triples in volume, about 6 minutes.

Fold chocolate mixture into whipped eggs with a flexible rubber spatula until completely incorporated.

Pour mixture into prepared pan. Bake for 22 minutes. The center will still be a little soft. Remove from oven. Let cool for at least 30 minutes before cutting. The center may ooze a little, which is wonderful. Serve warm, or refrigerate for up to 2 days and let sit at room temperature for at least 1 hour before serving.

SERVES 10

poached strawberries with sweet crème fraîche

Simplicity itself. Out-of-season straw-berries are transformed by a singular method into the most voluptuous fruit imaginable. They are sugared and left to sit in their own juices, and then stewed, albeit briefly, in these juices. Topped with a flourish of sweetened crème fraîche and a little berry with its green stem attached, it is a festive treat indeed. Serve with a Christmas cookie (page 71).

2 pounds ripe fresh strawberries

¾ cup plus 2½ tablespoons sugar

8 ounces crème fraîche

Wash strawberries and save 6 of the smallest for garnish. Remove stems from remaining strawberries and discard. Cut in half lengthwise and place in a large heavy saucepan. Pour ¾ cup sugar over strawberries and let sit for 30 minutes.

Bring strawberries just to a boil. Lower heat and simmer for 10 minutes, until the berries just begin to soften. Remove from heat. Let cool, then chill until ready to serve.

Meanwhile, put 2½ tablespoons sugar in a small bowl. Add 1 tablespoon boiling water and stir to dissolve. Mix into crème fraîche until smooth. Cover and refrigerate until crème fraîche thickens.

Distribute strawberries and liquid among 6 wine glasses, large martini glasses, or dessert coupes. Top with crème fraîche and a whole berry.

SERVE 6

slow-baked pears with stilton, warm honey syrup

This is a sophisticated cheese course that becomes dessert when paired with honey-roasted pears. Stilton is a blue-veined cheese from England, and a very merry one to eat this time of year alongside fruit dribbling with warm honey syrup. The pears can be made early in the day and kept at room temperature, with the syrup poured over before serving. Needless to say, the cheese should be served at room temperature for ultimate satisfaction along with some good port for sipping.

4 large firm ripe Comice or Bartlett pears

3 tablespoons plus ⅓ cup honey

6 ounces Stilton cheese

Preheat the oven to 400 degrees.

Peel pears using a vegetable peeler and cut in half lengthwise. Remove seeds using the small end of a melon baller. Heat 3 tablespoons honey and 2 tablespoons water in a 12-inch nonstick skillet until bubbly. Add pears, cut side down. Cook for 5 minutes, turn over, and cook for 3 minutes longer. Place cut side up on a rimmed baking sheet and add a little water to the bottom of pan. Bake until tender, about 35 minutes. Baste with pan juices halfway through cooking. Remove pears from oven and let cool.

When ready to serve, heat ⅓ cup honey and ⅓ cup water in a small saucepan until boiling. Lower heat and simmer for 10 minutes, or until reduced to ½ cup. Keep warm.

Place 2 pear halves on each of 4 large plates. Drizzle pears with warm syrup. Place a wedge of cheese next to pears and serve.

SERVES 4

christmas cookies

snowy shortbread

This is a wonderful basic butter cookie that you cut into myriad holiday shapes: stars, trees, and diamonds are nice. Let cool, then dust heavily with powdered sugar for a snowy look.

Preheat the oven to 300 degrees.

In bowl of an electric mixer, beat the butter until light and fluffy. Gradually add the confectioners' sugar and mix thoroughly. Stir in the flour and add a pinch of salt. Continue to mix until a smooth ball forms. Flatten into a disk, ⅓ inch thick. Wrap in plastic and refrigerate for 30 minutes.

Roll out the dough between ⅛ and ¼ inch thick on a board lightly dusted with flour. Using a variety of holiday cookie cutters, cut into shapes. Bake on an ungreased cookie sheet for about 25 minutes, or until cookies are dry but pale in color. Remove from oven and let cool on sheet. Sprinkle cookies heavily with confectioners' sugar pushed through a sieve.

MAKES ABOUT 36 (depending on size of cookie cutter)

2 sticks unsalted butter, at room temperature, cut into pieces

1 cup confectioners' sugar, plus more for dusting

2 cups all-purpose flour, plus more for dusting board

rainbow sugar cookies

This amazing little cookie puffs into an irregular slipper shape, which is part of its charm. More charming still is how the rainbow sugar makes you smile.

8 ounces mascarpone

1 cup all-purpose flour, plus more for dusting board

½ cup fine rainbow sugar*

Place mascarpone in bowl of an electric mixer. Stir in flour and a pinch of salt and mix briefly. Turn the dough onto a clean board, lightly dusted with flour, and knead just until smooth. Pat the dough into a ½-inch-thick circle and wrap in plastic. Refrigerate for 1 hour.

Preheat the oven to 450 degrees.

Using a small knife, cut dough into 24 to 26 squarish shapes. Using a rolling pin on a lightly floured surface, roll out the small pieces of dough until very thin in the shape of a slipper. Sprinkle each heavily with rainbow sugar. Place on a parchment-lined cookie sheet and bake for 12 minutes, until slightly puffed and golden. Let cool on a rack.

MAKES 24 TO 26

*Available in professional baking shops and many specialty food stores.

toasted almond cookies

Simple to make and more delicate than biscotti, these are especially delicious with fruit and chocolate desserts and not bad at all with a glass of Sauternes or Vin Santo.

Preheat the oven to 350 degrees.

In bowl of a food processor, process nuts until coarsely ground. You want some small, distinct coarse pieces, and some finely ground pieces. Place in a small nonstick skillet and heat, stirring constantly, until fragrant. Set aside.

Place egg whites in bowl of an electric mixer with a pinch of salt. Beat until just beginning to stiffen. Crumble in brown sugar and beat for several minutes, until stiff peaks form and the mixture is glossy. Gently fold in nuts with a flexible rubber spatula.

Line a baking sheet with parchment paper. Drop batter by the heaping tablespoonful onto parchment. Bake for 20 minutes, or until cookies are dark beige and just set. Remove from oven and let cookies cool on sheet. Store in a tightly covered tin.

MAKES 24

**2 cups
whole almonds**

**2 extra-large
egg whites**

**1 cup packed
dark brown sugar**

tiny macaroons

These taste nothing like those big wet macaroons we've all come to know. I like those, too, but these are more sophisticated. The secret is unsweetened dry coconut that resembles coarse white sand. It is available in health food stores and Middle Eastern markets. If you roll these very small, about the size of a large grape, they fit perfectly into 1-inch fluted paper cups and make lovely petits fours.

1½ cups packed unsweetened dessicated coconut, about 3 ounces

⅔ cup sweetened condensed milk

½ teaspoon rum extract

Preheat the oven to 375 degrees.

In a medium bowl, put coconut, condensed milk, rum extract, and a pinch of salt. Mix with a wooden spoon, making sure all the ingredients are combined. Let sit for 20 minutes so coconut absorbs some moisture.

Line a cookie sheet with parchment paper. Roll the dough into 20 to 22 small balls, making sure they are perfectly round. Place on parchment and bake for 18 minutes, until firm and just golden. Remove from oven and let cool on sheet. Store in a tin.

MAKES 20 TO 22

"cookies while you sleep"

'Tis just the recipe for the night before Christmas.

Preheat the oven to 375 degrees.

Beat egg whites until frothy. Add a pinch of salt and slowly add sugar. Beat for several minutes, until very stiff and glossy. The mixture should look like marshmallow fluff. Gently fold in 1 cup chocolate chips and drop by the tablespoonful onto a cookie sheet lined with parchment paper.

If desired, sprinkle a few of the remaining chips on tops of cookies, or on just half of the cookies for contrast. Place in oven on middle rack and turn oven off immediately. Leave door closed until morning. Merry Christmas

MAKES ABOUT 28

3 extra-large egg whites

⅞ cup sugar

1¼ cups miniature chocolate chips

on christmas morning

Freshly Squeezed Tangerine-
Pomegranate Juice with Orange-Flower Water

Thick-Cut Panettone French Toast

Cranberry-Maple Syrup

Five-Spice Bacon

Hot Chocolate from Paris

Strawberries with Mint Sugar

Almond Paste Chaussons

freshly squeezed tangerine- pomegranate juice with orange-flower water

During the holidays, I always have towering bowls filled with decorative tangerines around the house. And this is what I do after I'm through looking at them. It is a refreshing and exotic way to start the day. Get your kids to help you squeeze.

Cut tangerines in half through the equator and squeeze. You will have about 3½ cups juice. Put in a pitcher, add orange-flower water, and stir. Cut pomegranate in half and scoop out several tablespoons of seeds for garnish. Squeeze the juice from the pomegranate halves as you would squeeze oranges. Add to tangerine juice and chill well. Serve straight-up or on the rocks. Scatter seeds on top before serving.

12 large tangerines

2 teaspoons orange-flower water

1 large pomegranate

SERVES 4

thick-cut panettone french toast

Panettone is a cylindrical, slightly sweet, raisin-studded bread from Milan, and a culinary sign-post of festive holidays like Christmas. There are several good brands available in most supermarkets. Serve as is with an extra pat of butter or with the special Cranberry Maple Syrup, opposite.

1 small imported panettone (500 grams or 17.6 ounces)

6 extra-large eggs

6 tablespoons unsalted butter

Preheat the oven to 350 degrees.

Stand panettone upright. Cut thin slices of crust from opposite sides of panettone to "square it off" for easier slicing. Discard, save, or eat these pieces. Then, from top to bottom, cut the panettone into 6 slices of equal thickness (they should look like thick slices of sandwich bread). Place on a baking sheet and bake for 5 minutes so that panettone is lightly toasted and slightly dried out.

Meanwhile, beat eggs together with 3 tablespoons water in bowl of an electric mixer for several minutes, until light and fluffy. Place panettone in a large shallow casserole and cover with beaten eggs. Let sit for 10 minutes, turning once or twice, so that bread is soaked.

Heat 2 large nonstick skillets. Melt 2 tablespoons butter in each. Add 2 slices of panettone to each pan. Cook over medium-high heat for 5 minutes on each side, until golden. Place on a baking sheet. Repeat process, adding more butter as you go. When all the panettone is cooked and placed on baking sheet, put in oven and bake for 10 minutes, until puffy. Cut in half and serve 3 pieces per person. Serve immediately. Pass extra butter, if desired.

SERVES 4

cranberry-maple syrup

Place all the ingredients in a small heavy saucepan. Add ½ cup water and stir. Bring to a boil, then immediately lower heat and simmer for 15 minutes. Strain through a coarse-mesh sieve, pressing down on the cranberries to extract juice. Serve warm.

MAKES 1 CUP

1 cup fresh cranberries

1 cup pure maple syrup

1 cinnamon stick
or split vanilla bean

five-spice bacon

Preheat the oven to 375 degrees.

Carefully separate slices of bacon. In a small bowl, mix five-spice powder and confectioners' sugar. Sprinkle each slice lightly with mixture. Place on a large rimmed baking sheet. Bake for 15 minutes, then pour off fat. Bake for about 10 minutes longer, or until crisp. Remove from oven and let sit for 1 to 2 minutes before serving.

MAKES 16 SLICES

16 thick slices bacon,
about 1 pound

2 tablespoons
five-spice powder

4 tablespoons
confectioners' sugar

hot chocolate from Paris

This recipe comes from the venerable restaurant Ladurée in Paris by way of Dorie Greenspan, cookbook author extraordinaire, who lives in Paris and New York. We both think it's dreamy, especially on cold winter mornings when we're still in our robes.

3 cups whole milk

⅓ cup sugar

7 ounces best-quality bittersweet chocolate, chopped

In a medium saucepan, put milk, sugar, and ⅓ cup water. Cook over medium heat until just about boiling. Remove from heat and, using a wire whisk, whisk in the chocolate until smooth. If you have a hand-held or immersion blender, use it to whip the hot chocolate for 1 minute in the pan. If not, transfer the mixture to a blender and whip on high speed for 1 minute. Serve while it's very hot and frothy.

SERVES 4

strawberries with mint sugar

There is something mesmerizing about this combination of flavors, and it's refreshing, too. A nice counterpoint to the rest of this colorful Christmas breakfast.

3 pints ripe strawberries

½ cup sugar

2 bunches fresh mint

Wash strawberries and dry well. Remove the stems, reserving a few with stems for garnish. Cut stemmed strawberries in half through the stem end and place them in a pretty glass bowl.

Place sugar in bowl of a food processor. Wash mint and dry thoroughly. Make sure there is absolutely no water on the leaves. Chop enough to get ⅓ cup and add to the sugar. Process until mint is incorporated into the sugar. Cover strawberries with mint sugar right before serving. Garnish with remaining sprigs of mint and strawberries with stems.

SERVES 4 OR MORE

almond paste chaussons

These treats look like little gifts with slits that slyly reveal their contents. They are especially delicious to eat while you drink Hot Chocolate from Paris (see recipe on opposite page). Just dunk them in!

Thaw dough until pliable. Preheat the oven to 375 degrees.

Roll out dough so that it is about 10 by 12 inches. Cut into 6 even rectangles, about 4 inches wide and 5 inches long.

Crumble almond paste and place 1 tablespoon in a wide stripe down the length of each pastry a little to the right of center. Sprinkle with a little water and then with 1/4 teaspoon cinnamon-sugar. Fold over to make logs that are 2 inches wide and 5 inches long. Press edges tightly together, then crimp edges with the tines of a fork to make neat packages. Make 4 slits 1/2 inch from folded edge of pastry, about 1/2 inch apart, down the length of pastry.

Brush tops very lightly with water. Sprinkle pastries with remaining cinnamon-sugar, about 1/2 teaspoon each. Place on ungreased rimmed baking sheet and bake for 22 minutes, or until golden. Remove carefully with a spatula and let cool a bit before serving.

MAKES 6

1 sheet frozen
puff pastry, about
8¾ ounces

4 ounces almond paste,
about 6 tablespoons

2 tablespoons
cinnamon-sugar*

*You can
buy cinnamon-sugar
or make your own
by mixing
1 cup granulated
sugar with 1½
tablespoons
ground
cinnamon.

gifts from the kitchen

Cranberry and Sun-Dried Cherry Relish

14-Carrot Jam

Hard Sauce, a.k.a. Brandy Butter

White Chocolate–Peppermint Crunch

Fig "Salami" with Walnuts and Cardamom

Apricot Sweetmeats

Pignoli Brittle

cranberry and sun-dried cherry relish

This raw relish is also delicious cooked as a compote, which is another great gift. Make both!

Mix cranberries and sun-dried cherries in small bowl. Put half of mixture in bowl of a food processor. Process until coarsely but evenly chopped. Transfer to a bowl. Repeat with remaining mixture. Add brown sugar with a pinch of salt and a grinding of black pepper. Mix well so that all the sugar dissolves. Cover and let sit in refrigerator for at least 1 day before serving. Relish will keep for 1 week in refrigerator. Pack into glass jars as gifts.

MAKES 2½ CUPS

12 ounces cranberries, about 3 cups

4 ounces sun-dried cherries, about ¾ cup

¾ cup packed dark brown sugar

14-carrot jam

Peel carrots and grate on large holes of a box grater. You will have about 6 cups. In a heavy, medium pot, put carrots, sugar, lemon juice, and 2 cups water. Bring to a boil. Reduce heat and simmer for 1 to 1½ hours, or until syrup has thickened. Remove from heat and let cool. Sterilize four 8-ounce jelly jars in boiling water and dry thoroughly. Fill with jam, seal, and store in refrigerator. Keeps for months.

MAKES FOUR 8-OUNCE JARS

14 medium carrots, about 2 pounds

6 cups sugar

½ cup freshly squeezed lemon juice

hard sauce, a.k.a. brandy butter

Serve with steamed plum pudding, mince pies, or thin slices of fruitcake. Also spectacular with large ripe strawberries: Use a butter knife to spread a little on each berry.

6 tablespoons unsalted butter

1 firmly packed cup confectioners' sugar

2 to 3 tablespoons brandy

Bring butter to room temperature. Cream the butter in the bowl of an electric mixer, then add confectioners' sugar and mix. When smooth, slowly add the brandy and beat until creamy and pale. Put in a bowl or jar and refrigerate for at least 1 day. (If the butter starts to break, add a little more sugar.) Let come to room temperature before serving. Pack in a small crock as a gift.

MAKES 1 HEAPING CUP

white chocolate– peppermint crunch

8 ounces white chocolate

2 tablespoons white crème de menthe

⅓ cup coarsely crushed candy canes

Melt white chocolate in top of a double boiler over simmering water. Add crème de menthe, stirring until smooth. Spray a 7-by-7-inch pan with nonstick cooking spray and pour in mixture. Press crushed candy canes into mixture, distributing evenly. Chill and cut into squares. Line a box with colorful tissue paper and fill with candy as a gift.

MAKES 16 SQUARES

fig "salami" with walnuts and cardamom

Cardamom casts a spell with its mysterious fragrance. These are delicious with strong coffee. Wrap the "salamis" in fig or grape leaves for a great gift.

Cut figs in half and place in bowl of a food processor. Add 2 tablespoons water and process briefly. Add walnuts and a little more water if necessary to make a smooth, but not wet, paste. Remove from processor. Place on a piece of waxed paper and knead a few times. Roll into 2 logs, each 1⅓ inches in diameter and about 5 inches long. Roll each log in cardamom to coat completely. Chill for 4 hours or longer. Slice ¼ inch thick. Wrap tightly in fig or grape leaves and tie with raffia as a gift.

MAKES 16 SLICES

10 ounces
small dried black figs

½ cup finely chopped
walnuts, toasted

2 tablespoons
ground cardamom

apricot sweetmeats

24 small plump dried apricots

6 ounces almond paste, about 6 tablespoons

½ cup crushed pistachios

Freeze apricots. Remove from freezer and, using a small sharp knife, carefully cut each in half to make 2 equal circles so you can make a sandwich. Soften the almond paste with your fingers and place about 1 teaspoon on one apricot slice and flatten to make a filling about ⅛ inch thick. Top with another apricot half and press down hard. You want the filling to show all around the edges. Smooth the edges with a little water and then roll sides in crushed pistachios to coat completely. Line a small basket with lemon leaves and place sweetmeats inside. Wrap in cellophane and tie with ribbons as a gift.

MAKES 24

pignoli brittle

Put pignoli in a small nonstick skillet. Toast lightly over low heat, stirring often. Remove after a few minutes, when golden.

In a 12-inch nonstick skillet, put sugar and cloves. Melt sugar over medium-high heat, stirring constantly, until completely melted and dark brown. When all the sugar is melted and there are no lumps remaining, stir in pignoli to distribute evenly.

Spray a baking sheet with nonstick cooking spray or line with parchment paper. Immediately pour mixture onto sheet in a very thin layer, spreading with a wooden spoon to form a 9-by-10-inch rectangle. Let cool until hard. Break into pieces as desired. Line a pretty box with parchment paper and fill with brittle as a gift.

¾ cup pignoli (pine nuts)

1½ cups sugar

½ teaspoon ground cloves

MAKES ABOUT 14 OUNCES

a few holiday drinks

rosemary lemonade

This has just the right amount of sweet acidity and herbaceous perfume to make a suitable holiday drink without any alcohol.

6 large lemons

¾ cup sugar

1 small bunch rosemary

Cut 4 or 5 lemons in half and squeeze to get ¾ cup juice. Combine sugar, 1 cup water, and 1 tablespoon lemon juice in a medium saucepan. Add 2 tablespoons finely chopped rosemary. Mix well and bring to a boil. Remove from heat and let steep for 20 minutes. Pour through a fine-mesh sieve. Let syrup cool, then add 3 cups water and remaining lemon juice. Refrigerate until very cold. Serve in a pitcher over ice with lemon slices and sprigs of fresh rosemary.

SERVES 6

apples and anisette

This is a sophisticated drink and my favorite holiday cocktail.

1 lemon

½ cup fresh apple cider

1 tablespoon anisette

Remove long strips of lemon peel using a small sharp knife. Cut lemon in half and squeeze to get 1½ teaspoons juice. For each drink: Put 4 ice cubes in a large rocks glass. Add cider and anisette and stir. Add lemon juice and stir again. Garnish with lemon rind. Add a colorful stirrer.

MAKES 1 DRINK

This is addictive, and no one will guess the simple ingredients. Delicious hot or cold.

spiced red cider

Put apple juice in a nonreactive saucepan. Add cloves and bring to a boil. Lower heat and simmer for 10 minutes. Remove from heat and add tea bags. Let steep for 10 minutes. Remove tea bags and cloves. Gently warm before serving or serve chilled.

SERVES 4

1 quart apple juice

1 teaspoon
whole cloves

2 Red Zinger tea bags

Very elegant—it's worth buying large Martini glasses just for this.

"christmas-tini"

Make sure all your materials are chilled thoroughly, including large Martini glasses. For each drink: Pour schnapps into glass. Top with cranberry juice and float vodka on top. Serve with little green straws.

MAKES 1 DRINK

1 tablespoon
peppermint schnapps

½ cup cranberry juice

1 tablespoon vodka or
currant flavored vodka

A warming welcome drink for your guests.

cassis chaud

Put all the ingredients in a nonreactive saucepan with ⅓ cup water. Bring to a boil. Lower heat and simmer for 5 minutes. Serve warm. If desired, put a cinnamon stick in each small wine glass or cup and pour in hot drink.

SERVES 4

2½ cups Chardonnay

½ cup plus 2 tablespoons
crème de cassis

2 cinnamon sticks

three wise menus

Menus are narratives, tales to make us hunger. In the 1840s, during the time of Queen Victoria, guests celebrated Christmas with a noble baron of beef and an enormous plum pudding. One hundred and fifty years later, Julia Child feasted on roast double loin of pork with port wine sauce—and a golden roast capon for good measure. Nowadays, simplicity may be valued over flamboyance, but that doesn't have to mean giving up traditions. So I've designed three celebratory menus—with wine selections—to help you make the most of your time. In many homes, Christmas Eve custom dictates an all-fish dinner, while in others, roast goose is a ritual. And on Christmas Day, most everyone looks forward to a splendid ham taking center stage. I've also included a grand all-purpose holiday menu meant for any meal during the twelve-day celebration. It is unflaggingly English—bacon-wrapped oysters, prime rib, rutabaga mash, Stilton and pears—begging for a lovely glass of port and very good friends. For a special breakfast menu, turn to chapter 6,"On Christmas Morning." Of course, you may make your own menu magic with some of your family's own holiday favorites.

christmas
eve goose

As the moon glitters like a disco ball in a wintry sky, and plastic Santas dance between streetlamps, in the distance church bells shatter the night's silence. In your house, the fragrance of roasting chestnuts, ginger, and honey fill the air with delicious anticipation.

Angels and Archangels on Horseback (page 10)

Radish Wreath with
Goat Cheese and Toasted Cumin (page 9)

"Christmas-tini" (page 89)

Santa Claus Melon with Prosciutto (page 28)

Prosecco

Roast Goose with Chestnuts and Prunes (page 44)

Red Cabbage with Honey and Vinegar (page 52)

Sweet Potato–Ginger Puree (page 54)

Frenched Beans with Crushed Macadamia Nuts (page 55)

Côtes-du-Rhône or *Sangiovese*

Cider-Glazed Baked Apples with Marzipan (page 65)

Snowy Shortbread (page 71)

Calvados

a grand
christmas dinner

Much of this special dinner can be made ahead, so pour yourself a cup of good cheer and enjoy your company.

Golden Almonds with Dill (page 18)

Spiced Shrimp in Sweet Rice Wine (page 11)

Fino Sherry

Sweet Garlic-Fennel Bisque (page 25)

Sauvignon Blanc

Glazed Christmas Ham (page 46)

Sage-Roasted Capon with Wild Mushrooms (page 38)

Brussels Sprouts with Sun-Dried Cranberries (page 51)

Olive Oil Mashed Potatoes (page 56)

Ruby Beets and Beet Greens, Walnut Oil and Balsamic Syrup (page 61)

Pinot Noir

Heavenly Chocolate Cake (page 68)

Candy Cane Ice Cream (page 63)

Christmas Cookies (pages 71–75)

Brandy

english-style
holiday dinner

*This multi-course, all purpose menu dazzles with the generosity of the season
and the magic of 1–2–3.*

Stuffed Olives in Sweet Vermouth (page 18)

Angels and Archangels on Horseback (page 10)

Champagne, from an old vintage

Christmas Gravlax, Sweet Mustard Sauce (page 27)

Double Chicken Consommé with Sherry (page 26)

Prime Ribs of Beef, Cabernet-Garlic "Jus" (page 47)

Wild Rice with Five-Hour Onions (page 60)

Blasted Broccoli and Grape Tomatoes (page 57)

Rutabaga Mash with Glazed Shallots (page 58)

Claret or *Cabernet*

Slow-Baked Pears with Stilton, Warm Honey Syrup (page 70)

Store-Bought Fruitcake, Homemade Hard Sauce (page 84)

Port

index

radish wreath with goat cheese and toasted cumin

brie croustades with red caviar

santa claus melon with prosciutto

"a

b

s

le

spiced shrimp in sweet rice wine

slow-roasted tomato and watercress salad

double chicken consommé with sherry

christmas gravlax, sweet mustard sauce

sausages "al vino" with red and green grapes

ribs

ca

gar

smoked salmon in pillows

three-minute wasabi salmon

"three french he

hot and crispy cheese truffles

glazed christmas ham

brussels sprouts with sun-dried cranberries